NATIONAL GEOGRAPHIC

Wind

SHAPING EARTH'S SURFACE

Nash Kramer

PICTURE CREDITS

Cover: photograph of Pedestal Rock in New Mexico's Bisti
Badlands © Tom Bean/Corbis/Tranz.

Photographs: page 1, Corbis; page 4 (bottom left), Corbis; page 4
(bottom right), Photodisc; page 5 (top), Photodisc; page 5 (bottom
left), Photodisc; page 5 (bottom right), Corbis; page 6 © Michael S.
Yamashita/Corbis/Tranz; pages 7-8, Photodisc; page 9 © Bill
Ross/Corbis/Tranz; page 10 © Georges Gobet/Agence France
Presse; page 11 (top) © Reuters; page 11 (bottom), photo
courtesy USDA Natural Resources Conservation Service; page 12,
Photodisc; page 14 © Reuters; page 15 (top) © Wang
Chengxuan/Xinhua/AP Photo/AAP; page 15 (bottom), Corbis; page
16 © Hulton Archives/Getty Images; page 22 © Corbis/Tranz;
page 23, photo courtesy USDA Natural Resources Conservation
Service; pages 24-25 © Bettmann/Corbis/Tranz; page 26, photo
courtesy USDA Natural Resources Conservation Service; page 29
© Seth Joel/Taxi/Getty Images.

Illustrations on pages 13 and 19 by Kevin Currie.

Produced through the worldwide resources of the National
Geographic Society, John M. Fahey, Jr., President and Chief
Executive Officer; Gilbert M. Grosvenor, Chairman of the Board;
Nina D. Hoffman, Executive Vice President and President, Books
and Education Publishing Group.

PREPARED BY NATIONAL GEOGRAPHIC SCHOOL PUBLISHING
Ericka Markman, Senior Vice President and President, Children's
Books and Education Publishing Group; Steve Mico, Vice President
and Editorial Director; Marianne Hiland, Executive Editor; Richard
Easby, Editorial Manager; Jim Hiscott, Design Manager; Kristin
Hanneman, Illustrations Manager; Matt Wascavage, Manager of
Publishing Services; Sean Philpotts, Production Manager.

EDITORIAL MANAGEMENT
Morrison BookWorks, LLC

PROGRAM CONSULTANTS
Dr. Shirley V. Dickson, Program Director, Literacy, Education
Commission of the States; James A. Shymansky, E. Desmond Lee
Professor of Science Education, University of Missouri-St. Louis.

National Geographic Theme Sets program developed by Macmillan
Science and Education Australia Pty Limited.

Published by the National Geographic Society
1145 17th Street, N.W.
Washington, D.C. 20036-4688

ISBN: 0-7922-4746-9

Printed in China by The Central Printing (Hong Kong) Ltd.
Quarry Bay, Hong Kong
Supplier Code: OCP May 2018
Macmillan Job: 804263
Cengage US PO: 15308030

MEA10_May18_S

Contents

Shaping
Earth's Surface

Think of all the shapes and forms you can see on Earth's surface. These shapes and forms change all the time. Some changes happen quickly, as when an earthquake or volcano jolts the land. Other changes are slow, as when wind, water, or ice wears away rock. Wind, water, ice, earthquakes, and volcanoes are all forces that shape Earth's surface.

 ## Key Concepts ....

1. Different forces shape the landforms that make up Earth's surface.
2. Earth's surface changes in different ways.
3. People try to control, or at least understand, the effect of forces that shape Earth's surface.

Forces Shaping Earth's Surface

Wind

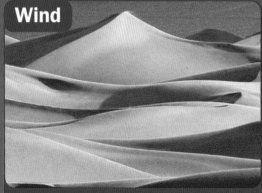

Wind can change the surface of rock, deserts, plains, and coastlines.

Water

Water can change the landscape by carving out canyons and valleys.

In this book you will learn how wind can wear away rock to change Earth's surface.

Ice

Ice can slowly change the shape of rock and create new landforms.

Earthquakes and Volcanoes

Earthquakes and volcanoes can build landforms and destroy them.

The Effects of Wind

Moving air is called wind. Wind can blow gently or with great strength. A gentle wind can make the weather pleasant. A strong wind can blow things over. It can move things from one place to another.

Wind can be very powerful. A strong wind can blow large amounts of soil from one place to another. Wind can even change the shape of the land.

Children in a strong windstorm in the country of Tibet

Key Concept 1 Different forces shape the landforms that make up Earth's surface.

Earth's Surface

Earth's surface, or outer layer, consists of rocks and soils. These rocks and soils make up **landforms**. Landforms are things like mountains, valleys, deserts, and plains. They give Earth's surface its shape.

Earth's surface changes all the time. Different **forces** cause these changes. Wind is one of these forces.

landforms
natural shapes on Earth's surface

forces
causes of movement and change

Mountains and deserts are landforms that help give Earth's surface its shape.

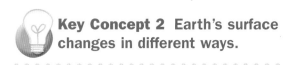

Key Concept 2 Earth's surface
changes in different ways.

How Wind Changes Earth's Surface

Different forces change the landforms on Earth's surface. Two of these forces are **weathering** and **erosion**. These forces cause change over time.

Weathering happens when rock slowly wears away. Wind is one cause of weathering. Wind can pick up bits of soil and sand and blow them against rock. This causes the rock to wear away. The rocks in this photograph have been weathered by the wind.

Rock shaped by wind at Bryce Canyon National Park in Utah

Erosion comes after weathering. It is a force that moves rocks and soils from one place to another. Wind can pick up worn-down rock **particles**. The wind then **deposits**, or drops, them in other places. Wind erosion can happen over a long time and over large distances. Sandstorms, dust storms, and coastal winds all change Earth's surface.

Wind erosion has shaped this landform at Arches National Park in Utah.

Sandstorms

Sandstorms can change Earth's surface very quickly. Sandstorms occur mainly in the desert. They happen when wind blows at speeds over 16 kilometers (10 miles) per hour. At this speed, wind can pick up the sand and move it. The stronger the wind, the farther it carries the sand. The force of the wind moves sand to a different place in the desert.

A truck is buried by sand after a sandstorm in Mauritania, Africa.

Dust Storms

Dust storms can also change the surface of Earth very quickly. A strong wind can pick up dry, fine soil. The wind can move the soil in the same way it moves sand. Dust storms happen where there are few trees and little grass. They also happen in places that have had little rain.

A dust storm slows down traffic in Beijing, China.

Wind has eroded most of the soil on this farm.

Coastal Winds

Winds blowing off the ocean can change landforms along the coast. These winds can form sand **dunes**. Ocean waves wash sand up onto a beach. Wind then blows the sand inland. The sand piles up against rocks and plants. The wind piles up more and more sand. Soon a hill of sand is formed. This hill of sand is called a dune.

Sand piles up against grasses. Over time, dunes are formed.

How Plants Keep Sand Dunes in Place

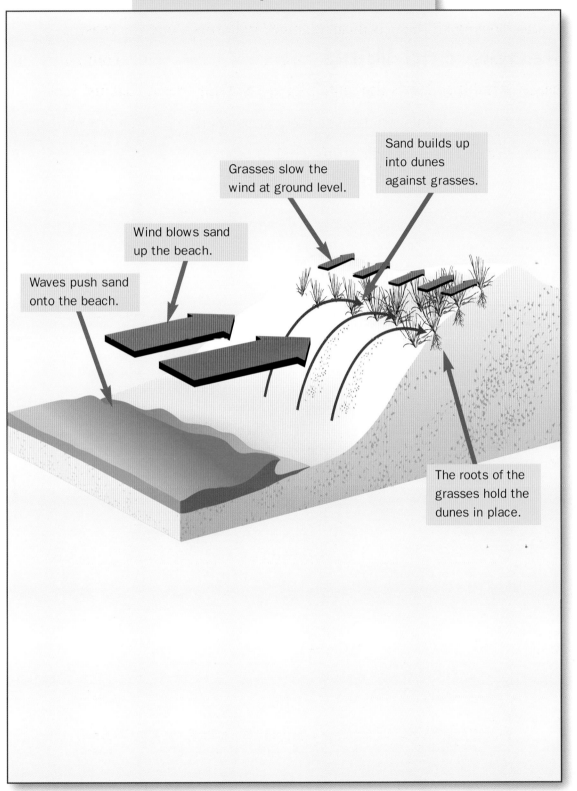

Waves push sand onto the beach.

Wind blows sand up the beach.

Grasses slow the wind at ground level.

Sand builds up into dunes against grasses.

The roots of the grasses hold the dunes in place.

Key Concept 3 People try to control, or at least understand, the effect of forces that shape Earth's surface.

People and Wind

Sometimes the **effects**, or changes, caused by wind can be harmful. Wind can damage the places where people live and work. People study wind to understand how it works. They try to prevent the damage it can cause.

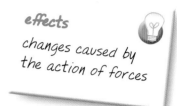

effects

changes caused by the action of forces

Sand dunes threaten a farm in China.

14

Desert Land

In China, sandstorms can change good land into desert. The winds in sandstorms lift and carry sand. The winds then dump the sand onto good land. Many plants can't grow well in sand. The effect is that much good land in China has become desert.

The Chinese government has started planting trees and grasses in desert areas that used to be good land. They hope that the roots of the plants will hold the sand in place. This will stop sand from being blown onto good farmland.

Farmers in China plant trees to hold the sand in place.

In China, the Gobi Desert is moving toward good land.

Lower Land Levels

Wind can make parts of Earth's surface lower. In the 1930s, there were dust storms on the Great Plains of the United States. The wind blew away the dusty soil. So much soil blew away that the level of the ground dropped. People helped stop the soil from being blown away. They planted rows of trees to slow the force of the wind.

These men are planting trees in Minnesota to prevent soil from being blown away.

Think About the **Key Concepts**

Think about what you read. Think about the pictures and the diagram. Use these to answer the questions. Share what you think with others.

1. Explain two ways that forces change Earth's surface.

2. Explain the difference between weathering and erosion.

3. In what ways can people be affected by the forces that shape Earth's surface?

4. In what ways can people control the effects of forces that shape Earth's surface?

Cutaway Diagram

Diagrams are pictures that show information.
You can learn new ideas without having to read many words.
Diagrams use pictures and words to explain ideas.

There are different kinds of diagrams.
This diagram of how trees form a wind barrier is a **cutaway diagram**. A cutaway diagram is a three-dimensional picture that shows a "slice" of something, such as a slice of Earth. Look back at the diagram on page 13. It is a cutaway diagram that shows how plants keep sand dunes in place.

How to Read a Diagram

1. Read the title.
The title tells you what the diagram is about.

2. Read the labels.
Labels point out the important parts of the diagram.

3. Study the diagram.
Which parts of the diagram are on the surface, and which parts are beneath the surface?

4. Think about what you learned.
What did the cutaway diagram show you?

How Trees Form a Wind Barrier

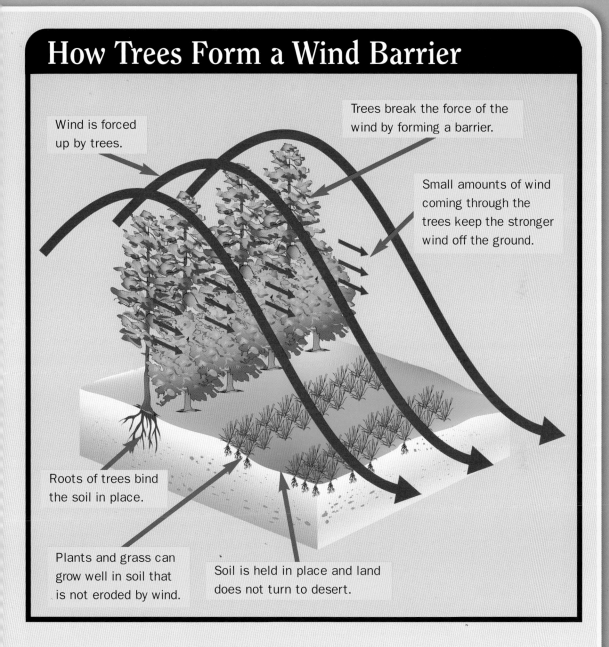

Wind is forced up by trees.

Trees break the force of the wind by forming a barrier.

Small amounts of wind coming through the trees keep the stronger wind off the ground.

Roots of trees bind the soil in place.

Plants and grass can grow well in soil that is not eroded by wind.

Soil is held in place and land does not turn to desert.

What Did You Learn?

Read the diagram by following the steps on page 18. Write a short paragraph explaining what you learned. Then exchange paragraphs with a classmate. See if your paragraphs are clear to each other.

Cause and Effect Article

Cause and effect articles may describe an event. They tell why the event happened (the causes) and the results of the event (the effects). The article starting on page 21 describes the Dust Bowl of the 1930s.

Cause and effect articles generally include the following:

The Introduction
The introduction gives general details about the event that will be described in the article.

The Body Paragraphs
The first few body paragraphs explain the causes and the next paragraphs describe the effects.

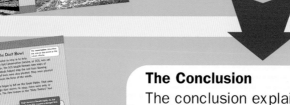

The Conclusion
The conclusion explains how the event ended or describes possible future effects.

The Dust Bowl

The **title** tells what the article will be about.

During the 1930s, wind caused a terrible problem in the United States. The area that was affected was the Great Plains. For many years little rain had fallen there. The ground became very dry, and the soil turned to dust. Then strong winds began to blow. The winds blew the dusty soil and created huge dust storms. Most states in the Great Plains were affected by the dust storms. The affected area became known as the "Dust Bowl." Oklahoma, Kansas, Colorado, New Mexico, and Texas had the most damage.

The **introduction** gives general details about the event.

Maps, photographs, or diagrams may support the text.

Dust Bowl Area

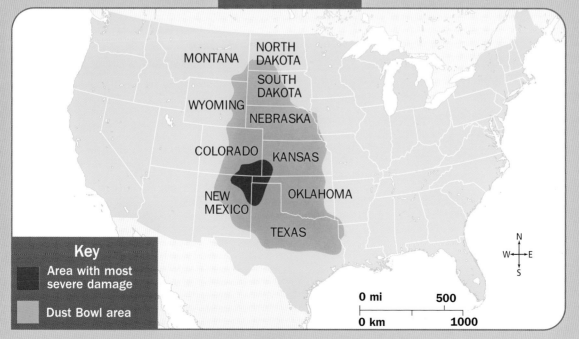

MONTANA
NORTH DAKOTA
SOUTH DAKOTA
WYOMING
NEBRASKA
COLORADO
KANSAS
NEW MEXICO
OKLAHOMA
TEXAS

N
W←→E
S

Key
Area with most severe damage
Dust Bowl area

0 mi ⊢————⊣ 500
0 km ⊢————⊣ 1000

Causes of the Dust Storms

First **body paragraphs** explain the causes.

The way people farmed land was one cause of the Dust Bowl. Grasses had once covered the land. These grasses did not need much rain. They had deep roots. The roots held the soil in place even when the wind blew. But farmers wanted to grow wheat on the land. They plowed up the grass and planted wheat instead. Wheat did not hold the soil in place as well as the grasses did.

Nature also helped to cause the Dust Bowl. There was not much rain for many years. The wheat crops dried up and died. There were few plants to hold the soil in place.

Then strong winds began to blow. They blew the dry soil into the air. This caused huge clouds of dust. During the 1930s, there were many dust storms. People called the dust storms "black blizzards."

A farm in the Dust Bowl, about to be hit by a dust storm

Effects of the Dust Storms

Next **body paragraphs** describe the effects.

The dust storms affected the lives of people in the Great Plains region. The wind blew the dust everywhere. The dust covered the land. It covered and killed plants. It covered roads. It blew into houses. The people were covered in dust. The dust was on their clothes. It was in their food and water. There was no escaping from it.

Effects on Farmers

The dust storms had a great effect on farmers. Farmers could not grow crops in the dust-covered fields. Many of their farm animals died from breathing the thick, dusty air. Other animals suffered from lack of food. Many farming families could not afford to keep their farms.

A farmer inspects his wind-eroded fields in the Dust Bowl of the 1930s.

Health Effects

The dust storms also had a serious effect on people's health. People breathed in the dust. This caused people to cough. It also made it difficult for them to breathe. Sometimes people developed a disease in their lungs. This disease was called dust pneumonia. Some people died from this disease.

Hospitals were set up to care for people. Masks were given to people living in the Dust Bowl region. The masks helped to filter out the dust.

These women are wearing masks to filter out the dust.

Leaving the Land

Because of the dust storms, many people moved from the Great Plains. They moved west to California in search of a better life. In 1935, 100 families left Texas County, Oklahoma, in just one month.

However, life in California was not easy. There were very few jobs available. Many people found themselves jobless and homeless. People from the Great Plains had led different lives from most Californians. Many found it hard to fit in. They became known as "Okies," whether they were from Oklahoma or not.

This man once owned a farm in Oklahoma. He moved to California and found work in this field, earning only 30 cents an hour.

The End of the Dust Bowl

The government needed to step in to help. A service called the Soil Conservation Service, or SCS, was set up in the mid 1930s. The SCS taught farmers new ways of farming. These methods helped stop the soil from blowing away. Thousands of trees were also planted. They were planted in short rows to break the force of the winds.

Then in 1938, rain began to fall on the Great Plains. That year, there were 61 large dust storms. In 1940, there were only 17 large dust storms. The time known as the "Dirty Thirties" had come to an end.

Hugh Hammond Bennett (right), the first chief of the SCS, inspects a damaged field.

Apply the Key Concepts

Key Concept 1 Different forces shape the landforms that make up Earth's surface.

Activity Draw a landscape with different landforms that are found on Earth's surface. Label the different landforms in your drawing.

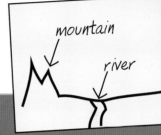

mountain

river

Key Concept 2 Earth's surface changes in different ways.

Activity Choose an example of weathering and erosion caused by wind. Then draw a simple diagram to show the steps in the process.

Sand Dunes
Waves wash sand onto beach

Key Concept 3 People try to control, or at least understand, the effect of forces that change Earth's surface.

Activity Imagine you are a person affected by wind erosion. Write a letter to a friend describing the changes brought about by wind and how it has affected you.

Dear Mary,

Write Your Own Cause and Effect Article

You have read the cause and effect article about an event in nature. Now you will write your own cause and effect article about an event you find interesting.

1. Study the Model

Look back at the description of cause and effect articles on page 20. Then read the introduction. What does it tell you about the topic? Read the body text. Think about how the information under the heading *Causes of the Dust Storms* is different from the information under the heading *Effects of the Dust Storms*. Now read the conclusion, *The End of the Dust Bowl*. Think about how the structure of this article helped you understand the topic.

Writing a Cause and Effect Article

◆ Choose an event with clear causes and effects.

◆ Write an introduction that gives general details about the event.

◆ Write "cause" paragraphs that tell why the event happened.

◆ Then write "effect" paragraphs that tell results of the event.

◆ Tell about the end of the event in your conclusion.

2. Choose Your Topic

Now choose an event in nature to write about. It should be an event that changed Earth's surface in some way, such as a landslide or an earthquake. You may find some ideas on the Internet or in books. Be sure to choose an event for which there are clear causes and effects.

3. Research Your Topic

Now that you have chosen your topic, you need to find more information about it. Use several different resources to find the information you need. Take notes as you come across important facts. Organize your information according to whether it is a cause or an effect.

Landslide

Cause: heavy rain

Cause: erosion

Effect: buildings destroyed

Effect: people killed

4. Write a Draft

Now it is time to write a draft of your article. First write the introduction. Give general information about the event, such as when and where it happened, how severe it was, and if people were affected. Write a section on the causes of the event and a section on the effects of the event. Finally, write a conclusion that explains how the event ended or describes possible future effects of the event.

5. Revise Your Draft

Read over what you have written. How clearly have you presented the information? Rewrite any unclear parts. Check against your research that all the facts you have included are accurate. Correct any spelling or punctuation errors that you find.

Create a
Cause and Effect
Chart

Follow the steps below to turn your article into a cause and effect chart. Then you can share your work with your classmates.

How to Make a Chart

1. Think of a heading.
Your heading should tell what the chart is about. Write the heading at the top of a large piece of paper.

2. Write down the causes.
Write the causes of the event in a list on the left-hand side of the piece of paper. You will not have much room for detail, so you will have to write brief notes. Draw a box around the list.

3. Write down the effects.
Write the effects in a list on the right-hand side of the piece of paper. Draw a box around the list.

4. Draw an arrow.
Draw an arrow across the page, linking the "causes" box to the "effects" box.

5. Illustrate your chart.
Add any diagrams or illustrations to make the text easier to understand.

6. Display your charts.
As a class, pin your charts to the classroom wall. Then move around the room, reading each other's charts. Be prepared to answer any questions about your chart.

Glossary

deposits – puts down or drops materials such as dust or rock particles

dunes – mounds of sand created by wind

effects – changes caused by the action of forces

erosion – the moving of worn-down rock and soil to another place

forces – causes of movement and change

landforms – natural shapes on Earth's surface

particles – very small pieces or parts

weathering – the wearing away of rock over time

Index